Instant Art for Bible Focus Sheets for Young People Book 1

Compiled by Susan Sayers
Illustrated by Fred Chevalier

First published in 1998 in Great Britain by
KEVIN MAYHEW LTD
Rattlesden
Bury St Edmunds
Suffolk IP30 0SZ

© 1998 Kevin Mayhew Ltd

Material in this book is copyright-free provided that it is used
for the purpose for which the book is intended. The usual
copyright restrictions apply to any use for *commercial* purposes.

Catalogue No 1396057
ISBN 1 84003 140 9

0 1 2 3 4 5 6 7 8 9

Illustrations by Fred Chevalier
Cover by Fred Chevalier
Printed in Great Britain

Contents

God is Near
- Receiving the Spirit — 1
- Led by the Spirit — 2
- Trusting God — 3
- Prayer — 4
- Daily quiet time — 5
- God hears our cries — 6
- Father, Son and Spirit — 7

Serving God
- When God calls — 8
- Faithful servants — 9
- Fight the good fight — 10
- Doing a good job? — 11
- With God's help — 12

Jesus
- Who was Jesus? — 13
- Epiphany — 14
- Simeon and Anna — 15
- Baptism — 16
- Temptation — 17
- Fishers of men — 18
- Jesus in the synagogue — 19
- Jesus – the Power of God — 20
- Jesus – the Word of God — 21
- The Transfiguration — 22
- Jesus is alive — 23
- Would you believe it? — 24
- Jesus is the Christ — 25
- Jesus is Lord — 26

The Good Life
- Sharing — 27
- The Beatitudes — 28
- True security — 29
- Rich and poor — 30
- Blessings — 31
- Saints — 32

Sin and Forgiveness
- What's wrong with me? — 33
- Think again — 34
- Get right with God — 35
- Lost and found — 36
- A fresh start — 37
- Made new — 38
- Love one another — 39

In Times of Trouble
- The cost of discipleship — 40
- When I feel down — 41
- Good out of evil — 42
- Costly love — 43

The Last Things
- Judgement Day — 44
- Christ is King — 45
- Heaven — 46

Bible Reference Index

Reference	Page	Reference	Page	Reference	Page
Genesis 1:1-4	21	Matthew 2:1-12	14	John 14:8-11	21
Genesis 2:4b-25	20	Matthew 6:6	5	John 14:16-19, 22-26	2
Genesis 3:8-11	36	Mark 12:26-27	46	John 20:1-18	23
Genesis 11:1-9	1	Luke 2:22-40	15	John 20:19-31	24
Genesis 15:1-7	3	Luke 2:41-52	13	John 20:29	46
Exodus 13:2, 12	15	Luke 3:15-17, 21-22	16	Acts 2:1-4	1
Deuteronomy 7:9-11	36	Luke 4:1-13	17	Acts 3:19	37
1 Kings 17:7-16	12	Luke 4:14-30	19	Acts 5:27-33	24
1 Kings 19:14	41	Luke 5:1-11	18	Acts 9:36-43	25
2 Kings 2:1-14	8	Luke 6:20-26	28	Acts 16:6-10	2
2 Kings 5:1-14	38	Luke 6:27-38	39	Acts 16:16-34	26
Nehemiah 8:1-3, 5-6, 8-10	19	Luke 7:11-13	12	Romans 7:21-25a	33
Psalm 17	46	Luke 7:36-50	33	Romans 8:10-11	46
Psalm 18:6	6	Luke 8:22-25	20	1 Corinthians 15:35-37, 54	46
Psalm 30	12	Luke 9:28-36	22	2 Corinthians 4:16-18	46
Psalm 32	33, 37	Luke 10:25-37	35	2 Corinthians 5:10	37
Psalm 43	41	Luke 11:1-13	4	2 Corinthians 5:17	38
Psalm 46	45	Luke 12:13-21	29	2 Corinthians 13:14	7
Psalm 51	36	Luke 14:12-14	27	Galatians 5:25	46
Psalm 65	31	Luke 14:25-33	40	Philippians 2:5-8	13
Psalm 80	10	Luke 15:1-10	36	Philippians 3:8, 10	42
Psalm 102	6	Luke 16:19-31	30	Philippians 3:20-21	46
Psalm 139	40	Luke 17:5-10	9	Colossians 1:9-12	32
Psalm 146:5-9	12	Luke 17:11-19	6	Colossians 3:23-25	11
Isaiah 1:10-18	37	Luke 18:1-8	5	1 Timothy 6:12	10
Isaiah 6:5	18	Luke 18:9-14	31	2 Timothy 3:16, 17	5
Isaiah 43:18, 20, 21	42	Luke 19:1-10	37	Hebrews 1:1-3	21, 10
Isaiah 53:4-6	36	Luke 21:5-19	44	Hebrews 4:14-16	17
Isaiah 66:23	14	Luke 24:1-12	23	Hebrews 13:16	27
Jeremiah 17:5-8	28	Luke 24:36-45	46	James 1:27	36
Jeremiah 18:1-6	40	John 1:1-18	21	1 Peter 5:8, 9	10
Lamentations 3:19-23	9	John 3:5-6, 16	46	1 John 1:1-4	36
Ezekiel 34:26	31	John 4:23-24	46	1 John 5:11-12	46
Hosea 6:1-6	36	John 10:11	36	Revelation 4	20
Amos 7:7-8, 10-17	35	John 11:22-30	25	Revelation 10	25
Malachi 4:1-2	44	John 13:31-35	43	Revelation 11:15-18	45

General Index

Topic	Page	Topic	Page	Topic	Page
Abraham	3	Heaven	25, 46	Spirit	1, 2, 7
Amos	35	Incarnation	13	Suffering	42
Authority	5, 20	John the Baptist	16, 34	Tabitha	25
Brother David	3	Miracle	12, 18, 20, 25, 38	Temple	13, 15
Church	12	Mother Theresa	3	Temptation	17
Community	27	Naaman	38	Thanks	6
Corrie Ten Boom	3, 39	Paul	26	Thomas	24
Creation	20, 21	Peace	10	Trust	3, 12
Cross	40, 43	Prayer	4, 5, 6, 7, 11	Vocation	8
Death	23, 46	Repentance	15, 33, 37	Wealth	28, 29, 30
Elijah	8, 12, 41	Reign	26, 45	Wise Men	14
Example	32	Resurrection	23, 24	Word	20, 21
Excuses	34	Sad	41	Work	11
Faith	3, 12, 24	Satan	10	Worship	23, 45
Forgiveness	33, 34, 37, 39	Signs	25	Zacchaeus	37
Happiness	28	Sin	33, 34, 35, 37		

Led by the Spirit (John 14:16-19, 22-26)

Focus Sheet 2

Trusting God (Genesis 15:1-7) — Focus Sheet 3

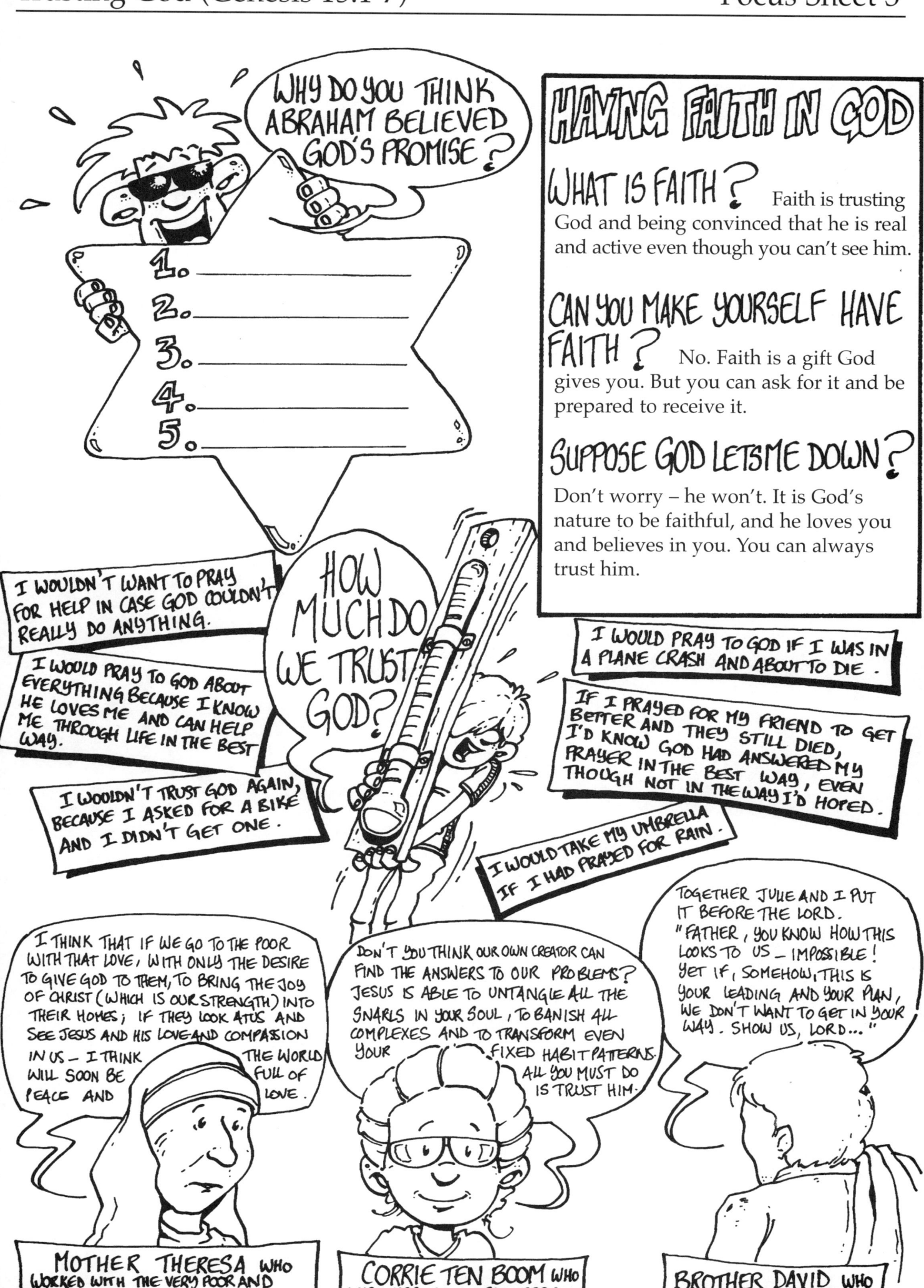

Prayer (Luke 11:1-13)

Focus Sheet 4

God hears our cries (Psalm 18:6) — Focus Sheet 6

Father, Son and Spirit (2 Corinthians 13:14)   Focus Sheet 7

God is the Holy Trinity

When God calls
Focus Sheet 8

2 Kings 2.1-14
What's in a mantle?

What did Elisha ask to inherit?

"_ _ O _ E _ O _ _ _   O _ E _ I _ _ ' _   _ _ I _ I _"
(verse 9)

On what condition could he have it?

"I _ _ O _   _ E E _ E _ E _ I   _ _ E _ _ O _ _ O ,   I _ _ _ E _ _ O _ ."
(verse 10)

To Pray...

Your ways, O God, are holy.
What God is so great as our God?
You are the God who performs miracles;
You display your power among the peoples.

Being Called
What's a vocation?

It's when you sense God wanting you to do a particular work. It's stronger than just liking the idea of it.

Can you feel called when you're a child?

Oh yes. Lots of people have known since they were children that God wanted them to be priests or missionaries or relief workers, as well as do other jobs.

How does God call someone?

He can speak into your thoughts and feelings. It may happen when you have been praying, it may be through something you see, and you know it's for you.

An Interview

YOU: How long have you been a priest / youth worker / lay preacher?

THEM:

YOU: How did your calling happen?

THEM:

YOU: What kind of commitment does there have to be?

THEM:

YOU:

THEM:

Faithful servants (Luke 17:5-10)   Focus Sheet 9

LORD, REMEMBER MY SUFFERING AND HOW I HAVE NO HOME.
REMEMBER THE MISERY AND THE SUFFERING.
I REMEMBER THEM WELL AND I AM VERY SAD.
BUT I HAVE HOPE WHEN I THINK OF THIS:
THE LORD'S LOVE NEVER ENDS.
HIS MERCIES NEVER STOP.
THEY ARE NEW EVERY MORNING.
        (— FROM LAMENTATIONS —)

THE STRENGTH TO SUFFER

I WOULDN'T CHOOSE TO SUFFER.
Neither would I! Jesus doesn't ask us to be masochists. But sometimes our work as Christians may bring us suffering.

WHY?
It may mean standing up for what is right, or pointing out wrong in our society. Or saying 'no' to some luxuries or some relationships that we'd like.

HOW CAN I GET GOD'S STRENGTH TO HELP ME?
Just ask for it. It's free. And God will always give you enough for the job.

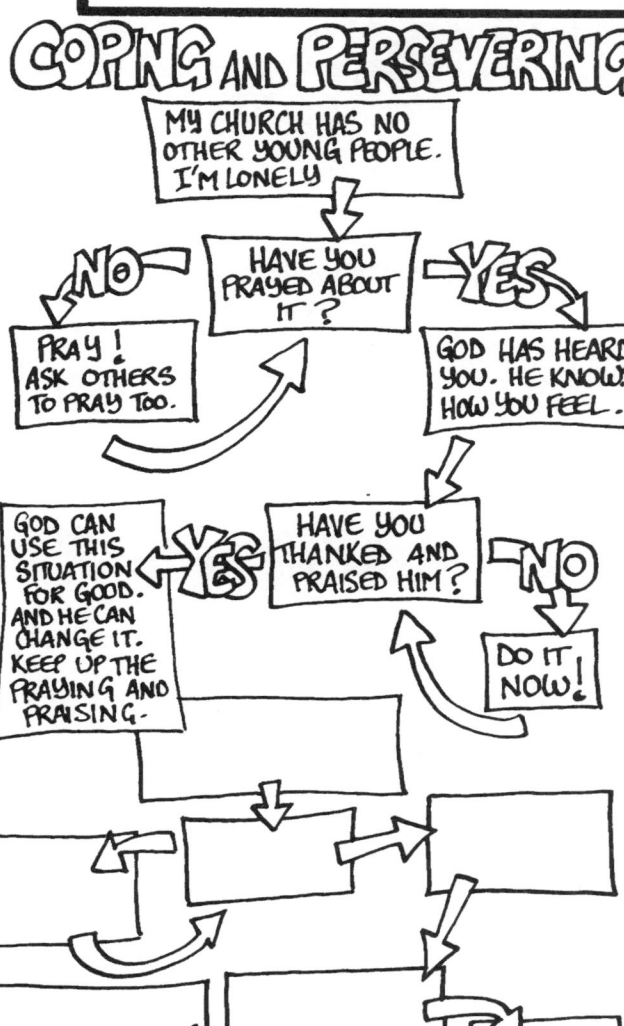

Who was Jesus? (Luke 2:41-52)

Focus Sheet 13

WHAT QUESTIONS MIGHT JESUS HAVE BEEN WONDERING ABOUT HIMSELF AS HE HEARD THE TEACHERS?

INCARNATION

WHAT DOES IT MEAN? Being embodied in flesh, or God becoming human as Jesus.

WHY DID GOD BECOME HUMAN? So he could share our humanity and we could see what God is like in human terms.

DID JESUS REALISE WHO HE WAS? When he was 12 years old he spent a long time listening and asking questions at the temple. Gradually he was understanding where he fitted into God's plan. He probably went on understanding more about it all his life, right up to the crucifixion and resurrection.

WELL WORTH LEARNING BY HEART!!!

PHILIPPIANS 2 v. 5~8

Your attitude should be the same as that of Christ Jesus:
who, being in very nature God
did not consider equality with God
something to be grasped,
but made himself nothing,
taking the very nature of a servant,
being made in human likeness.
And being found in appearance as a man,
he humbled himself
and became obedient to death –
even death on a cross!

INCARNATION AT BETHLEHEM!

AN HONOUR — EXCITING — LONELY — CRAZY — DIFFICULT — HUMBLING

WHAT MUST THIS HAVE FELT LIKE FOR JESUS?

CIRCLE ANY YOU AGREE WITH AND ADD YOUR OWN IDEAS!

Epiphany (Matthew 2:1-12) Focus Sheet 14

THE QUEST
WISE MEN FROM THE EAST COME TO FIND JESUS

What helped them to find him?

What threatened to make it fail?

Why did they set off on such a journey?

EPIPHANY

WHAT DOES 'EPIPHANY' MEAN?
It comes from Greek and it means being shown, or revealed, or manifested.

WHO WAS BEING REVEALED?
Jesus was being revealed to the Gentiles of other countries.

WHAT IS A GENTILE?
Someone who is not Jewish.

WHAT WAS THE STAR THEY SAW?
Some people think it was a comet, but others think it was two of the planets (Saturn and Jupiter) which were very close at that time.

'All nations will come and bow down before me.' Isaiah 66.23

Traditionally, the gifts have come to mean this:

GOLD — A sign of kingship and purity of character

FRANKINCENSE — A sign of prayer and worship to God

MYRRH — A sign of suffering and human death

PRAYER FOR THE WORLD
LORD JESUS CHRIST SON OF THE LIVING GOD HAVE MERCY ON US.

Baptism — Focus Sheet 16

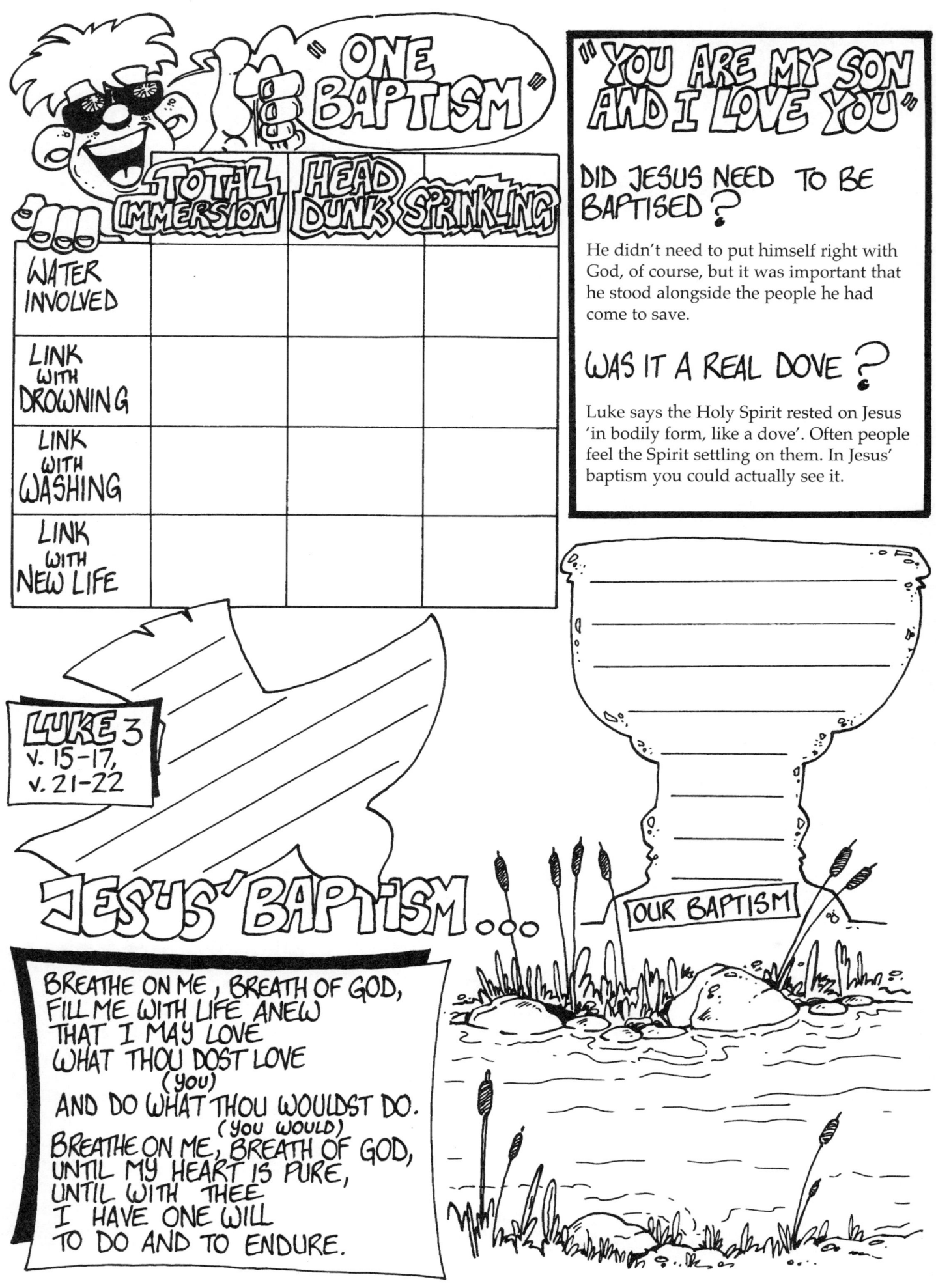

"ONE BAPTISM"

	TOTAL IMMERSION	HEAD DUNK	SPRINKLING
WATER INVOLVED			
LINK WITH DROWNING			
LINK WITH WASHING			
LINK WITH NEW LIFE			

"YOU ARE MY SON AND I LOVE YOU"

DID JESUS NEED TO BE BAPTISED?

He didn't need to put himself right with God, of course, but it was important that he stood alongside the people he had come to save.

WAS IT A REAL DOVE?

Luke says the Holy Spirit rested on Jesus 'in bodily form, like a dove'. Often people feel the Spirit settling on them. In Jesus' baptism you could actually see it.

LUKE 3 v. 15-17, v. 21-22

JESUS' BAPTISM...

OUR BAPTISM

BREATHE ON ME, BREATH OF GOD,
FILL ME WITH LIFE ANEW
THAT I MAY LOVE
WHAT THOU DOST LOVE
(you)
AND DO WHAT THOU WOULDST DO.
(you would)
BREATHE ON ME, BREATH OF GOD,
UNTIL MY HEART IS PURE,
UNTIL WITH THEE
I HAVE ONE WILL
TO DO AND TO ENDURE.

Temptation (Hebrews 4:14-16)   Focus Sheet 17

COUNT ME OUT! HOW GOOD ARE YOU AT STANDING UP FOR WHAT YOU BELIEVE?

1. IN A DISCUSSION GROUP AT SCHOOL EVERYONE TAKES FOR GRANTED THAT TEEN MAG MORALS ARE FINE. YOU DISAGREE. DO YOU...
   A. KEEP QUIET SO THEY WON'T LAUGH AT YOU?
   B. AGREE, SO YOUR FRIENDS COUNT YOU IN WITH THEM?
   C. TAKE A BIG BREATH AND SAY WHAT YOU THINK?

2. AT THE DISCO YOUR FRIENDS ARE TRYING TO IMPRESS ANOTHER GROUP BY MOUTHING OFF IN WAYS YOU FIND REALLY OFFENSIVE. DO YOU...
   A. JOIN IN ANYWAY, RATHER THAN BE THOUGHT WEIRD?
   B. TRY TO GET THEM INTERESTED IN DANCING INSTEAD?
   C. ASK THEM TO STOP AS IT UPSETS YOU.

3. A GROUP OF YOUR FRIENDS ARE PLANNING TO GO OUT TOGETHER ON A SUNDAY MORNING. DO YOU...
   A. AGREE, RATHER THAN LET THEM KNOW THAT YOU USUALLY GO TO CHURCH?
   B. MAKE FAMILY VISITORS AN EXCUSE SO YOU CAN GO TO CHURCH WITHOUT THEM KNOWING
   C. SUGGEST A LATER TIME, AS YOU'LL BE IN CHURCH ON SUNDAY MORNING - THEY'RE WELCOME TO COME WITH YOU IF THEY WANT!

THE TEMPTATIONS

WHO? Jesus was tempted by Satan.

WHEN? Just after he had been baptised.

WHERE? In the wild country where Jesus had gone to fast and pray.

WHAT? 'Make these stones bread.'
'I'll give you these kingdoms if you worship me.'
'Do something dramatic like jumping off the top of the temple. They'll follow you if you're a super-hero.'

Luke 4:1-13

HOW DID YOU DO???

Mostly A's: HARD ISN'T IT? BUT GOD NEEDS PEOPLE LIKE YOU BECAUSE YOU'RE PROBABLY SENSITIVE AND NON-THREATENING. WATCH OUT FOR THE OPPORTUNITIES HE GIVES YOU.

Mostly B's: YOU KNOW WHERE YOU STAND WITH GOD. THAT'S GREAT BUT YOU ARE A BIT SCARED OF YOUR FRIENDS. LET THEM SEE THE REAL YOU SOMETIMES - THEY MAY NOT BE AS HORRIFIED AS YOU THINK.

Mostly C's: WELL DONE FOR STANDING UP FOR WHAT YOU BELIEVE SO BRAVELY! BUT BE CAREFUL THAT YOU ALWAYS RESPECT WHERE OTHER PEOPLE ARE COMING FROM.

LEAD US NOT INTO TEMPTATION BUT DELIVER US FROM EVIL. AMEN

Fishers of men (Luke 5:1-11) Focus Sheet 18

"WHY WAS ISAIAH SO UPSET? FILL IN THE REST (ISAIAH 6:5)"

"WOE IS ME! I AM RUINED!"

SIMON PETER

WHO WAS HE?
He was a fisherman who lived at the same time as Jesus was teaching.

PLACE OF WORK.
The sea of Galilee.

WORK PARTNERS.
He owned a boat with his brother, Andrew. Two brothers in another family (James and John) worked with them on big hauls.

HOW HE MET JESUS.
He let Jesus sit in his boat to teach the crowds one morning.

THE FOLLOW ME GAME

Before you start, make some fish cards

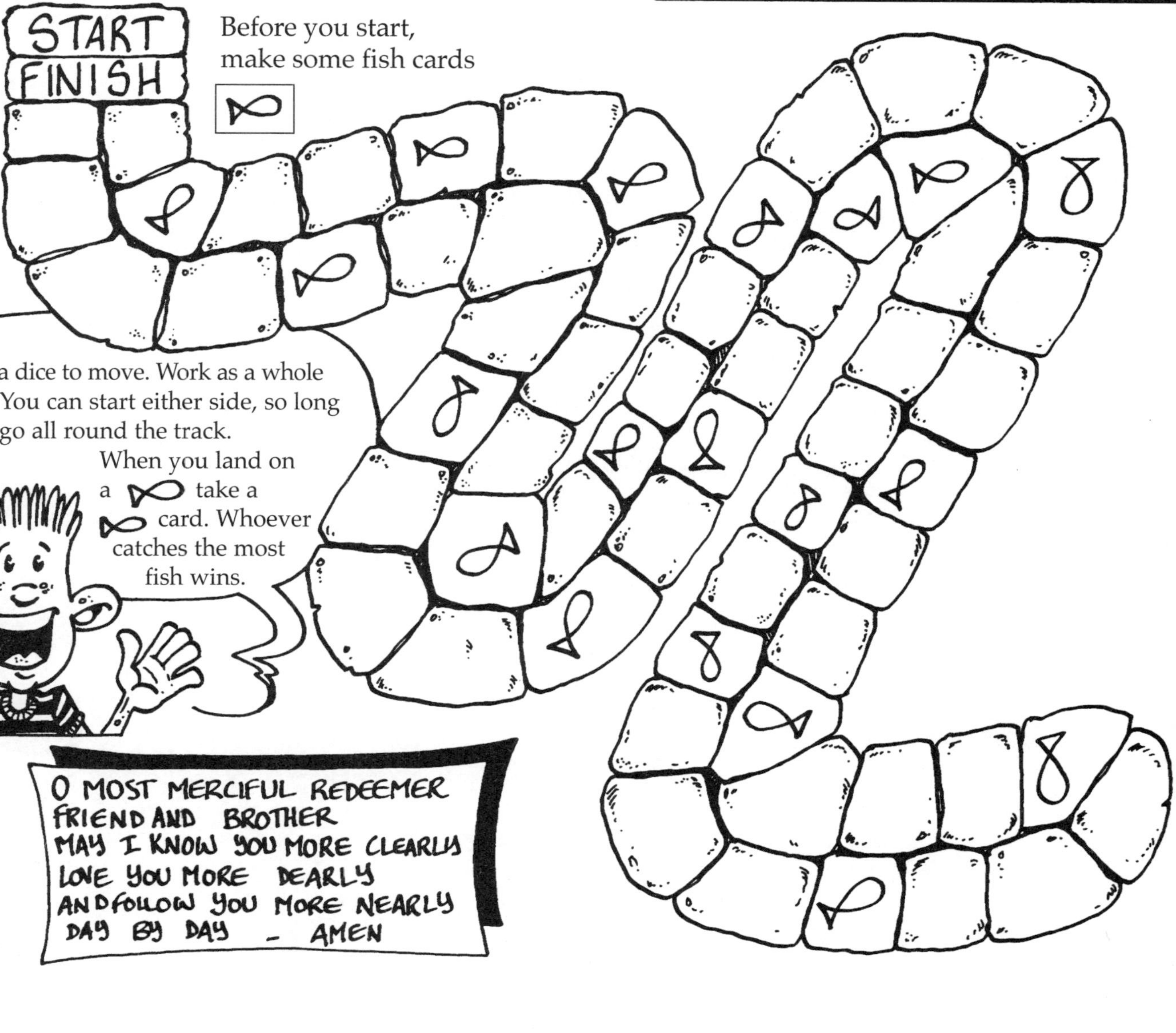

Throw a dice to move. Work as a whole group. You can start either side, so long as you go all round the track. When you land on a 🐟 take a 🐟 card. Whoever catches the most fish wins.

O MOST MERCIFUL REDEEMER
FRIEND AND BROTHER
MAY I KNOW YOU MORE CLEARLY
LOVE YOU MORE DEARLY
AND FOLLOW YOU MORE NEARLY
DAY BY DAY — AMEN

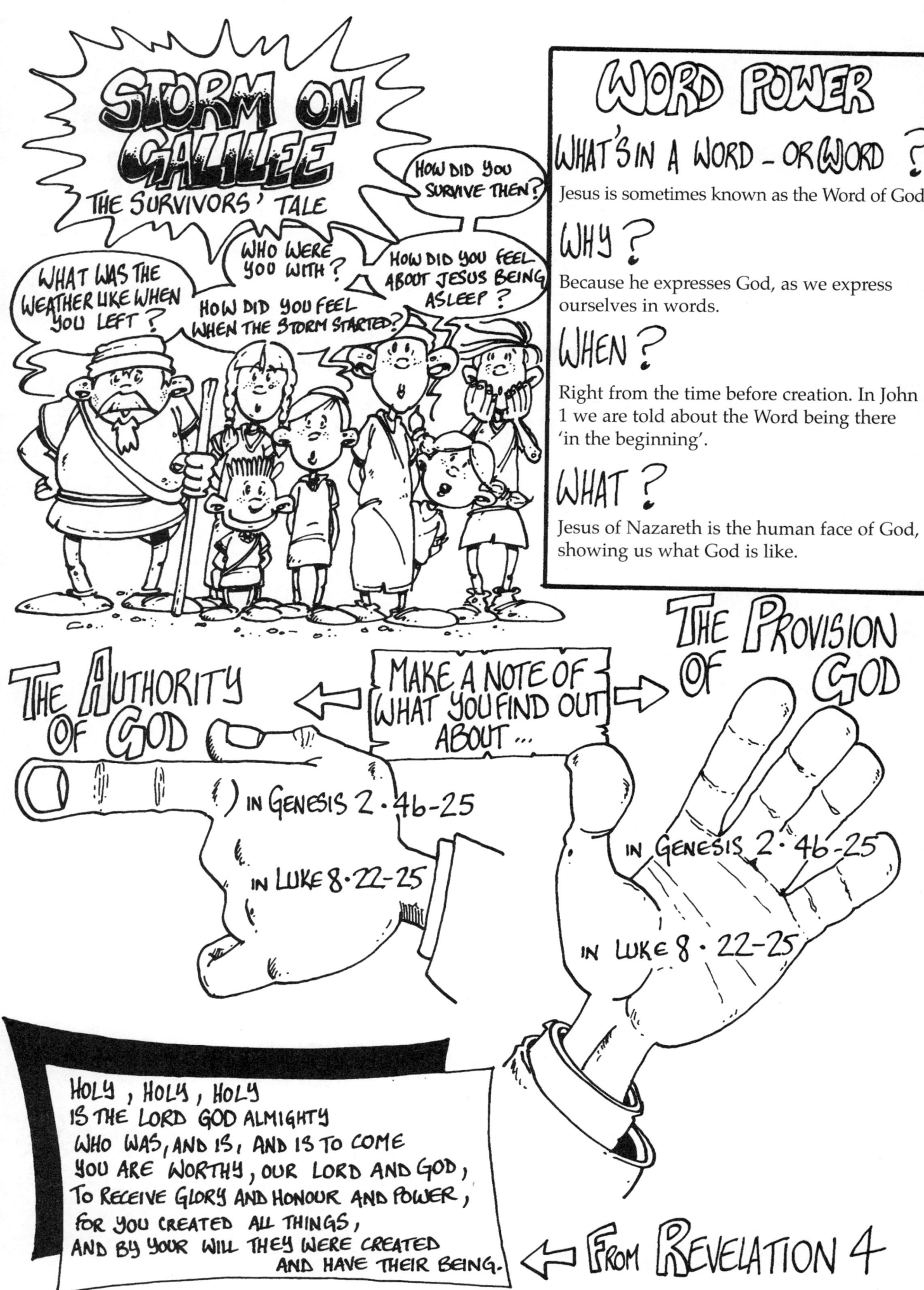

The Transfiguration (Luke 9:28-36) — Focus Sheet 22

Would you believe it? (John 20:19-31) — Focus Sheet 24

Sharing — Focus Sheet 27

ANNE: Right then, who are we going to invite?
GEORGE: Tom, Pete, Vanessa, Sam — if we don't invite them they'll cut us dead. And that's 4 parties we'll get invited back to.
ANNE: O.K. We'll put them down. What about Alison and Sarah?
GEORGE: No — last time they didn't give us anything. John always gives good presents, though. He's rolling in it.
ANNE: (writing) John. He's certainly worth having.
GEORGE: There's Matthew. He never gets asked to anything and he'd enjoy our party.
ANNE: Mmm, that's true. But he'd turn up wearing his school uniform or something and the others would think we were soft inviting him.
GEORGE: Yeah, we can't really invite Matthew, can we? He wouldn't fit in.
ANNE: And it's our party. We can invite whoever we want...
ANNE and GEORGE: ...can't we?

LIVING GOD'S WAY

WHY IS GOD'S WAY BEST?

God's way of life is what we were made for, so we work best as individuals and as a community if we live this way.

WHAT IF I WANT TO DO THINGS MY WAY?

You're free to choose that way — God will never force us to live lovingly, but he hopes we will because he knows it will make us happy.

YOU SAID COMMUNITIES ARE BETTER LIVING LIKE THIS. HOW?

If a whole community decides to look after one another's needs and live unselfishly, just think how safe and healthy and freeing it will be.

LUKE 14 v. 12-14 — WHO SHALL WE ASK?

Lord, may I show my love for you in the way I treat other people. Teach me your ways and encourage me to stick with them.
Help me get my motives right so I'm doing right things for the right reasons.
— AMEN —

HEBREWS 13 v 16 — WHY BOTHER?

WHAT KIND OF PARTY?   WHEN AND WHERE?

WHAT ABOUT A PARTY?

The Beatitudes

Focus Sheet 28

True security (Luke 12:13-21)

Focus Sheet 29

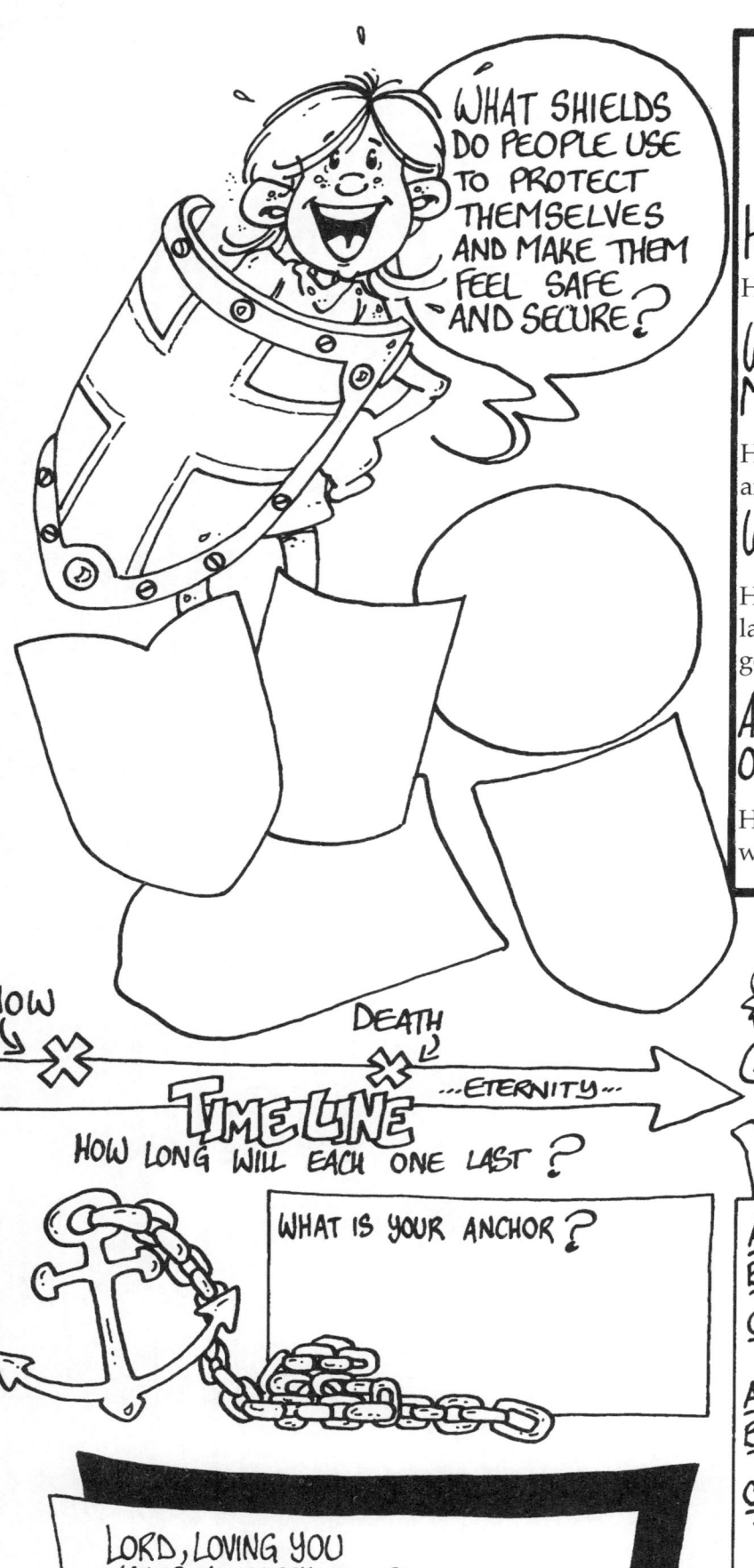

WHAT SHIELDS DO PEOPLE USE TO PROTECT THEMSELVES AND MAKE THEM FEEL SAFE AND SECURE?

THE FOOLISH RICH MAN

HOW DID HE GET RICH?
He had a huge bumper harvest.

WHAT DID HE DO WITH THE MONEY?
He kept it all so he could do what he liked and have a good time.

WHY WAS HE FOOLISH?
He forgot that this world's wealth doesn't last beyond death, and he didn't bother to get rich spiritually.

AT LEAST HE COULD ENJOY YEARS OF HAPPINESS FIRST?
He died that night. We never know when we will die. It's wise to be prepared.

NOW — DEATH — ETERNITY
TIME LINE
HOW LONG WILL EACH ONE LAST?

WHAT IS YOUR ANCHOR?

A. I'VE GOT A NEW BIKE WITH 36 GEARS.
B. WELL, I NEED A NEW BIKE WITH 36 GEARS. I'LL ASK MY PARENTS.
C. WHY SHOULDN'T I STEAL A BIKE? I'LL NEVER HAVE THE MONEY TO BUY ONE.

A. I'M GOING TO FLORIDA AGAIN THIS YEAR.
B. WE COULD GO TO FLORIDA IF I PERSUADED MUM TO WORK MORE HOURS.
C. IT'S NOT FAIR. EVERYBODY ELSE GOES TO FLORIDA. WE STAY WITH NAN AT CLACTON.

A. I AM A RICH FOOL.
B. I AM AN ENVIOUS FOOL.
C. I AM A RESENTFUL FOOL.

A, B, C. AND WE'RE ALL TRAPPED BY MONEY!

LORD, LOVING YOU MAKES ME HAPPY AND FREE.
NO MONEY CAN BUY THAT.
YOUR OFFER IS A COMPLETE BARGAIN—
THANK YOU FOR GIVING ME
WHAT I COULD NEVER EARN.
—AMEN—

Rich and poor (Luke 16:19-31)

Focus Sheet 30

- WALLS TO BLOCK OFF THE WORLD
- WEALTHY TRENDY FRIENDS
- NO MONEY WORRIES
- COMFORTABLE HOME
- PLENTY OF FOOD

HOW DID THE RICH MAN'S WEALTH MAKE IT HARD FOR HIM TO TAKE NOTICE OF LAZARUS'S NEEDS?

TAKE ME, LORD, AND TRAIN ME. LET ME NOT TRUST THE PROTECTION OF WEALTH AND RISK BECOMING HARDENED TO THE NEEDS AROUND ME.
INSTEAD, GIVE ME YOUR PROTECTION WHICH KEEPS ME ETERNALLY SAFE BUT ALLOWS ME TO FEEL AND SUFFER WITH THE SUFFERING WORLD, AND WORK TO RELIEVE IT.
— AMEN —

HOW RICH IS RICH?

DOES BEING A CHRISTIAN MEAN I'VE GOT TO BE POOR?

No. But it does mean that your money does what you want it to instead of it controlling your life.

IT'S HARD NOT TO GET CAUGHT UP IN SPENDING, THOUGH.

Yes, you're right. Living more simply will probably be hard, and your friends may think you're weird, giving money away instead of spending it on yourself.

THERE'S SO MUCH REAL POVERTY IN THE WORLD. HOW CAN MY MONEY HELP?

If we all gave some, and shared our world's resources more fairly, there would be enough for everyone.

WHERE DO YOU COME IN THE WEALTH SCALE?

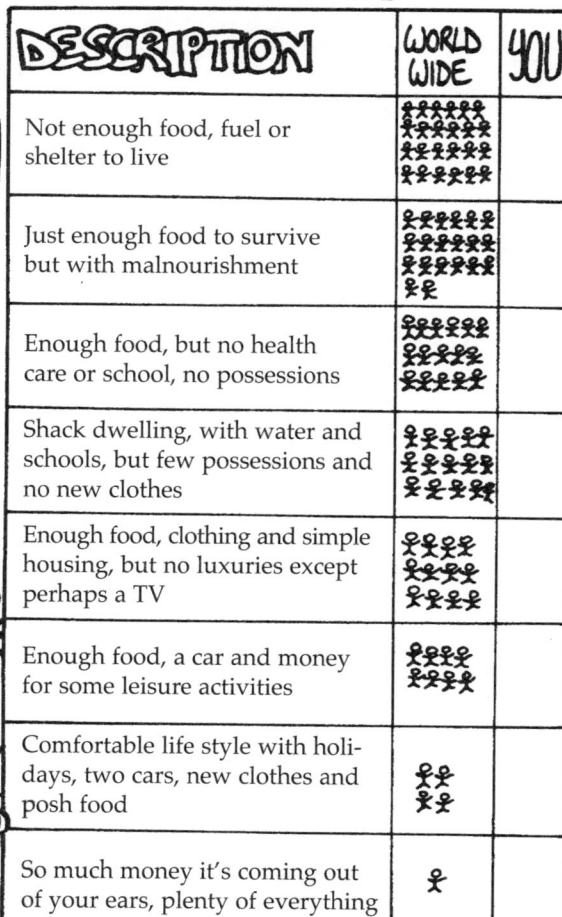

WHAT DOES THIS SAY ABOUT YOUR RESPONSIBILITIES?

Description	World Wide	You
Not enough food, fuel or shelter to live	👤👤👤👤👤👤 👤👤👤👤👤👤 👤👤👤👤👤👤 👤👤👤👤👤👤	
Just enough food to survive but with malnourishment	👤👤👤👤👤👤 👤👤👤👤👤👤 👤👤👤👤👤👤 👤👤	
Enough food, but no health care or school, no possessions	👤👤👤👤👤👤 👤👤👤👤👤 👤👤👤👤👤	
Shack dwelling, with water and schools, but few possessions and no new clothes	👤👤👤👤👤 👤👤👤👤👤 👤👤👤👤👤	
Enough food, clothing and simple housing, but no luxuries except perhaps a TV	👤👤👤👤 👤👤👤👤 👤👤👤👤	
Enough food, a car and money for some leisure activities	👤👤👤👤 👤👤👤👤	
Comfortable life style with holidays, two cars, new clothes and posh food	👤👤 👤👤	
So much money it's coming out of your ears, plenty of everything	👤	

(ROUGHLY)

Blessings (Ezekiel 34:26) Focus Sheet 31

"THESE ARE SOME OF THE BLESSINGS GOD SHOWERS ON US:"

WHAT STOPS US FROM RECEIVING THEM

IN LINE FOR GOD'S BLESSING

HOW DO WE GET IN LINE?
Look at your life measured against God's rule of love, and sort out what needs sorting. Tell God you are sorry and ask for his help.

WHAT'S THE BLESSING?
I can't tell you exactly because it will be exactly what you need. (God knows you a lot better than I do!)

GIVE ME SOME EXAMPLES.
O.K. Courage, peace of mind, bubbling joy, quiet joy, hope and reassurance, understanding about someone or something, healing, complete forgiveness, the knowledge that God really does know and love you ... and lots more!

"GOD, HAVE MERCY ON ME, A SINNER." — THE TAX COLLECTOR

"GOD, I THANK YOU THAT I AM NOT LIKE OTHER MEN — ROBBERS, EVILDOERS, ADULTERERS —"

"— OR EVEN LIKE THIS TAX COLLECTOR. I FAST TWICE A WEEK AND GIVE A TENTH OF ALL I GET." — THE PHARISEE

LUKE 18 v. 9-14

Prayer Hints I Picked Up From These Two:

1.
2.
3.
4.

YOU ANSWER US IN AMAZING WAYS, GOD OUR SAVIOUR.
PEOPLE EVERYWHERE ON EARTH AND BEYOND THE SEA TRUST YOU.
YOU TAKE CARE OF THE LAND AND WATER IT.
YOU MAKE IT VERY FERTILE.
THE RIVERS OF GOD ARE FULL OF WATER.
(— FROM PSALM 65 —)

Saints (Colossians 1:9-12)

Focus Sheet 32

Called to be Saints

WHO, ME?

That's right. In Christ we are all called to be filled with God's Spirit and live in his strength. Saints are people who do this. In the Bible the people of God in the Church are sometimes called 'the saints of God'.

WILL I GET A HALO, THEN?

The ring of light painted in pictures round the heads of holy people was drawn as a symbol of their lives 'shining' with God's love. God hopes you will shine, but it probably won't show as a gold band round your head. (But you could try wearing a shampoo shield.)

HOW CAN MY LIFE SHINE?

With joy, love, hope, patience, kindness, peace, self-control, goodness and gentleness.

THANKS BE TO YOU, MY LORD JESUS CHRIST,
FOR ALL THE BENEFITS WHICH YOU HAVE GIVEN ME;
FOR ALL THE PAINS AND INSULTS
WHICH YOU HAVE BORNE FOR ME.
MOST MERCIFUL REDEEMER, FRIEND AND BROTHER.
MAY I KNOW YOU MORE CLEARLY,
LOVE YOU MORE DEARLY
AND FOLLOW YOU MORE NEARLY,
DAY BY DAY.
(FROM ST RICHARD OF CHICHESTER'S PRAYER)

What's wrong with me? (Romans 7:21-25a)   Focus Sheet 33

ME AND MYSELF

Me	I can't believe I really did that. How can I live with myself?
Myself	Well, don't believe it. Tell yourself you didn't do it.
Me	But I did do it. It was awful. It brings me out in a cold sweat just thinking about it.
Myself	Tell yourself you couldn't help it.
Me	OK, I couldn't help it. Why couldn't I help it?
Myself	All that pressure from the others, remember. And you're still getting over a cold.
Me	Yes, that's true. I was a bit run down, wasn't I?
Myself	Of course you were. And it isn't as if you make a habit of behaving like that. It's just one of those things that happen. You can't blame yourself.
Me	No, I can't, can I? It wasn't my fault at all, was it?
Myself	And look at the terrible things you read about. What you did wasn't nearly as bad as that.
Me	That's right. It was nothing compared with that. Nothing at all.
	(Slow knocking at the door)
Outsider	May I come in? I have something important to show you. It's a matter of life and death.
Me	Yes, sure, come in. I've got nothing to hide. What's that you're holding?
Outsider	A mirror of the soul. It reflects not your outer body but your inner self. There, look into it. What do you see?
Me	Aaagh! *(Cries as if in pain)* It is myself, but not the self I want to be! It is the truth, but not the truth I want to see! Oh God, I have sinned. Have mercy on me!

RECOGNISING SIN

WHAT IS SIN? Sin is thinking, speaking or behaving in a way that is alien to loving God and loving one another.

IF SIN IS HORRIBLE WHY DO WE DO IT? It doesn't feel horrible at first. It feels nice to gossip about someone, and indulge yourself without control and so on. But in the long run it damages you.

HOW? Every time you sin and don't put it right you walk further away from God's presence. Like walking away from a bonfire, you get colder and deeper in darkness.

HOW CAN I PUT IT RIGHT? Tell God you are sorry. Turn round and walk back to him. He will welcome you with open arms and forgive your sin completely.

To Pray Whenever you need to

HAPPY IS THE PERSON WHOSE SINS ARE FORGIVEN, WHOSE WRONGS ARE PARDONED.
WHEN I KEPT THINGS TO MYSELF, I FELT WEAK DEEP INSIDE ME.
THEN I CONFESSED MY SINS TO YOU. I DIDN'T HIDE MY GUILT.
AND YOU FORGAVE MY SIN.
YOU ARE MY HIDING PLACE.
YOU PROTECT ME FROM MY TROUBLES.
YOU FILL ME WITH SONGS OF SALVATION!
(FROM PSALM 32)   — AMEN —

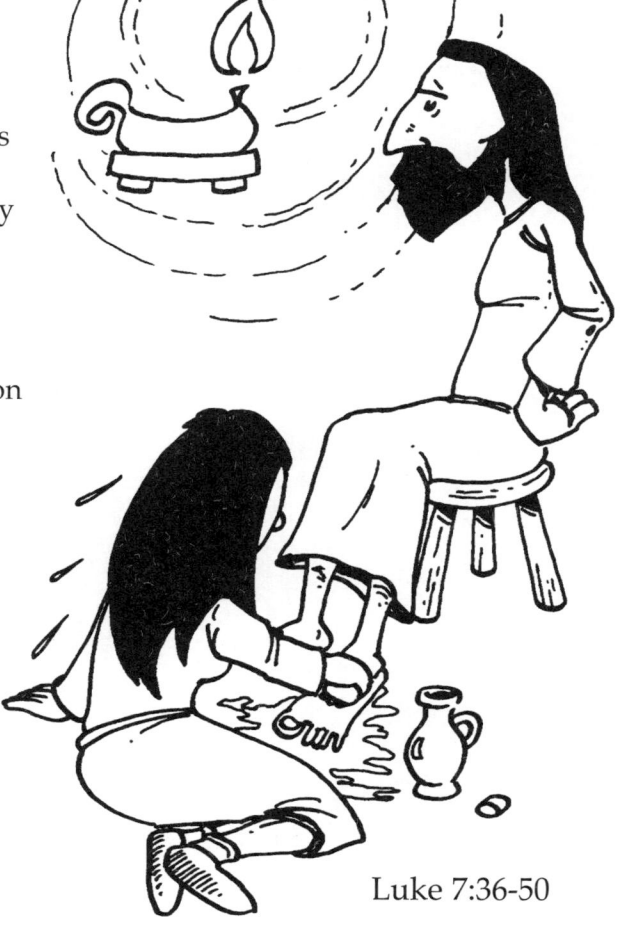
Luke 7:36-50

Think again (Luke 3:7-18)

Focus Sheet 34

Lost and found (Luke 15:1-10)

Focus Sheet 36

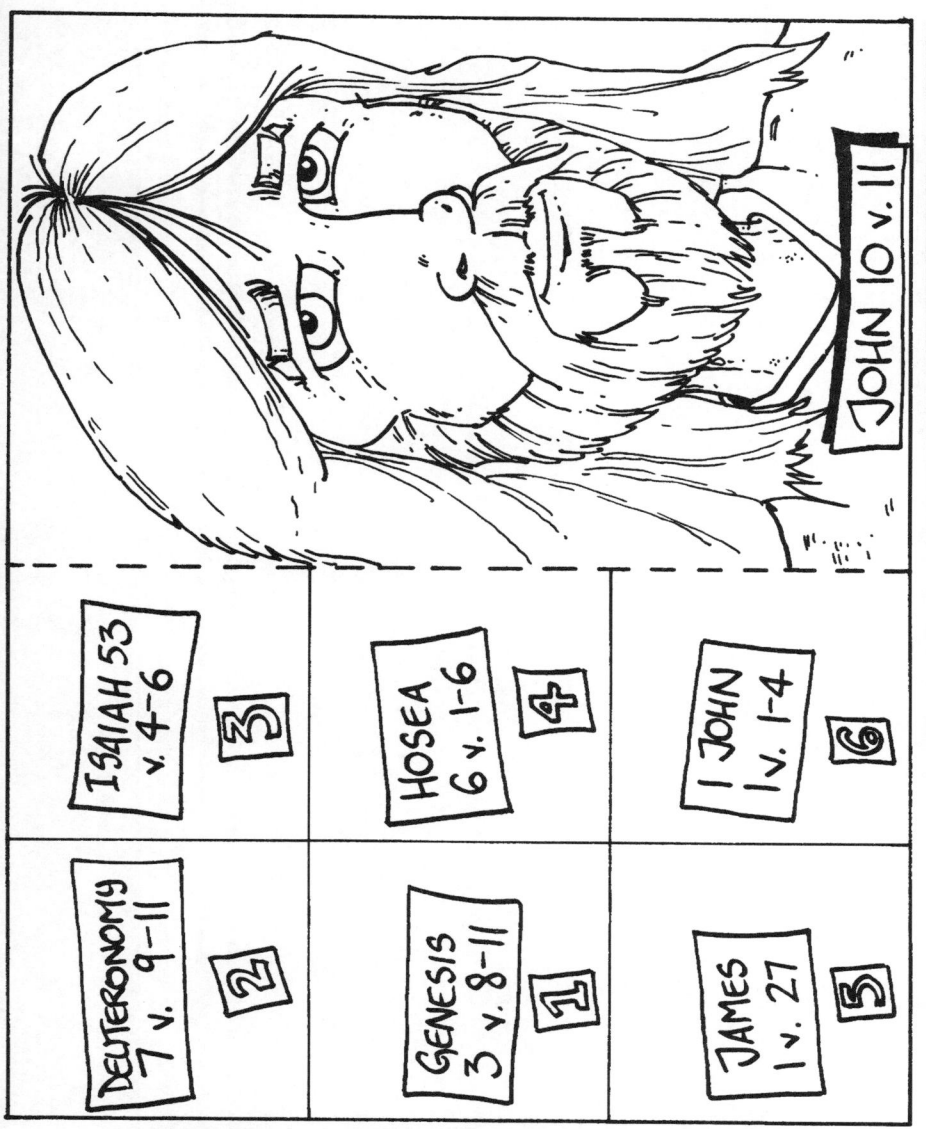

LOST AND FOUND

WHO ARE THE SHEEP AND THE COIN? Anyone who drifts or turns away from God and cuts themselves off from him.

WHY DOESN'T GOD STOP THEM? Because he loves them so much that he leaves them free to choose. Sometimes they make wrong choices.

HOW DOES HE FIND THEM? I'VE NEVER SEEN HIM LOOKING. He uses lots of ways. He can use our friends and enemies, TV programmes, events at school and work, music, holidays, visits. Even a smile.

COLOUR THE PICTURE, FOLD AND STICK TOGETHER THE 2 BLANK SIDES AND CUT INTO THE 6 PIECES SHOWN. EACH DAY THIS WEEK, READ THE PASSAGE FROM THE BIBLE AND TURN THAT PIECE OVER TO SHOW A BIT OF THE PICTURE. BY NEXT SUNDAY YOU WILL HAVE THE WHOLE PICTURE OF JESUS.

O GOD, IN YOUR KINDNESS HAVE MERCY ON ME, AND IN YOUR COMPASSION BLOT OUT MY OFFENCE. WASH ME AND WASH ME FROM ALL OF MY GUILT AND CLEANSE ME FROM ALL OF MY SIN.
(— FROM PSALM 51 —)

WHY DO 'SHEEP AND COINS' GET LOST?

A fresh start (Luke 19:1-10)   Focus Sheet 37

Love one another
Focus Sheet 39

LOVE ONE ANOTHER
Mum is putting the cleaner away. Dad is reading the sport page. Katrina is making her face up in front of the mirror. Michael walks in...

MUM: Hey, watch where you put your muddy feet — I've just cleaned that floor.

MICHAEL: That's right — shout at me as soon as I put my face round the door.

DAD: Don't you talk to your mother like that, young man. I won't have it.

(Michael sees Katrina in his sweater)

MICHAEL: Who said she could wear my sweater?

KATRINA: (sighs) I only borrowed it. (She takes it off) Here, catch. Have it back. It smells.

MICHAEL: Cheek! It's better than the stinky perfume you're wearing. Skunk, is it?

MUM: Oh shut up, everyone. I can't stand living like this. Let's start again.

(They all walk backwards to their starting place)

HOW DO YOU THINK IT WOULD GO IF EVERYONE WAS LIVING BY JESUS' TEACHING IN LUKE 6.27/38?

CORRIE TEN BOOM

BORN In Holland, the daughter of a clock maker and seller.

IMPRISONED By the Nazis in Ravensbruck women's concentration camp.

BELIEVED Completely in Jesus' power to save and forgive and set free.

WITNESSED To many in the camp and afterwards in prisons all over the world. 'At that moment, when I was able to forgive, my hatred disappeared.'

LIVING IN A FORGIVING WAY...

AT HOME IN THE MORNING

AT SCHOOL

WITH FRIENDS

This prayer was found near a child's body in Ravensbruck women's concentration camp. How does it make you feel?

O Lord, remember not only the men and women of good will but also those of evil will. But do not remember all the suffering they have inflicted upon us; remember the fruits we have borne, thanks to this suffering: our comradeship, our loyalty, our humility, our courage, our generosity, the greatness of heart which has grown out of all this; and when they come to judgement, let all the fruits we have borne be their forgiveness.

The cost of discipleship (Luke 14:25-33)   Focus Sheet 40

Good out of evil
Focus Sheet 42

CROSS-WORD!

1. 'Do not dwell on the _ _ _ _ _' Isaiah 43 v 18
2. 'I consider all the things I used to take pride in as _ _ _ _ _ _ _ _' Philippians 3 v 8
3. '_ _ _ _ _ _ the former things' Isaiah 43 v 18
4. 'I provide water for the people I _ _ _ _ _ _ for myself' Isaiah 43 v 21
5. 'And _ _ _ _ _ _ _ in the wasteland' Isaiah 43 v 20
6. 'That they may proclaim my _ _ _ _ _ _' Isaiah 43 v 21
7. 'That I may gain _ _ _ _ _ _ _' Phil. 3 v 8
8. 'The fellowship of _ _ _ _ _ _ _ _ in his sufferings' Phil. 3 v. 10
9. The opposite of evil.
10. Christ can bring ⑨ out of this!!!

CAN SUFFERING EVER BE GOOD?

SURELY SUFFERING IS JUST BAD? It certainly hurts, and we don't go looking for it. But...

BUT WHAT? God really can use even things like suffering for good.

HOW? It can teach us about patience, giving up possessiveness, and teach us to lean on God in the way we live.

IS THERE SOMETIMES WIDER GOOD, TOO? Yes. People who have suffered may bring about political and social changes for good.

CAN SUFFERING ALWAYS BE USED THEN? Yes. But if we choose to turn it into resentment and bitterness we waste any good that could have come.

WHAT GOOD CAN GOD BRING FROM THIS?

Lord, was I really worth dying for?
Can you really love me that much?
I know I can't earn your forgiveness
however many services I go to
and however many prayers I say
but you forgive me for free
just because you love me!
That's amazing!!!
   Amen.

LORD, HAVE MERCY!

Costly love (John 13:31-35) — Focus Sheet 43

Christ is King (Revelation 11:15-18) — Focus Sheet 45

FLAG MAKING STARTS HERE!

1. You'll need a length of lining material, about 1 meter square (minimum) and a bamboo cane.

2. Fold the side edge over the stick and either sew or staple it securely.

3. Have a practice at flag waving to some music — the larger the sweep, the better. Try dancing while you wave it.

4. Try a sequence with several of you — flag waving together!

CHRIST IS KING

WHERE IS CHRIST'S KINGDOM?
You can't catch a plane or boat to it, because it isn't a particular place on earth. Christ's kingdom is wherever Christ is allowed to reign as King.

I'VE ASKED JESUS TO BE LORD OF MY LIFE, SO DOES THAT MEAN THE KINGDOM IS IN ME? That's right. It's in you and all the others who put God first. It's in every situation where God reigns.

WE NEED THAT KINGDOM IN THE IMPORTANT INTERNATIONAL CONFERENCES. We certainly do. That's why we pray for all leaders and their meetings.

HOW COULD JESUS GO ON FORGIVING EVEN WHEN HE WAS DYING ON THE CROSS? IT MUST HAVE BEEN SO HARD. That's love for you.

God is our refuge and strength, an ever-present help in trouble. Therefore we will not fear, though the earth give way and the mountains fall into the heart of the sea, though its waters roar and foam and the mountains quake with their surging. "Be still, and know that I am God". (from Psalm 46)

"GOD AND SINNERS RECONCILED" MEANS...

DICTIONARY

RECONCILED: v. to be brought together in harmony again. For a close relationship to be healed. People who had been cut off from each other are joined again. Communication channels are opened up again.

Heaven
Focus Sheet 46